So...
You want to work in
TV?

So...
You want to work in
TV?

Alan Quays

KOGAN PAGE

YOURS TO HAVE AND TO HOLD
BUT NOT TO COPY

First published in 1998

Apart from any fair dealing for the purposes of research or private study, or criticism or review, as permitted under the Copyright, Designs and Patents Act 1988, this publication may only be reproduced, stored or transmitted, in any form or by any means, with the prior permission in writing of the publishers, or in the case of reprographic reproduction in accordance with the terms and licences issued by the CLA. Enquiries concerning reproduction outside those terms should be sent to the publishers at the undermentioned address:

Kogan Page Limited
120 Pentonville Road
London N1 9JN

© Alan Quays, 1998

The right of Alan Quays to be identified as author of this work has been asserted by him in accordance with the Copyright, Designs and Patents Act 1988.

British Library Cataloguing in Publication Data

A CIP record for this book is available from the British Library.

ISBN 0 7494 2758 2

Typeset by JS Typesetting, Wellingborough, Northants.
Printed in England by Clays Ltd, St Ives plc.

Contents

1	Glamour, glitz and grind	1
2	Sleeping your way to the top (and other partial myths)	11
3	How to win jobs and influence programmes	21
4	The future presentation	37
5	What's on the other side?	43
Appendix: For what it's worth		49

1

Glamour, glitz and grind

Television is one of the most attractive areas to work in. Since the small screen now occupies a central position in everyone's household and in everyone's life, the idea of getting on the other side of it is extremely alluring. TV programmes are the subject of everyday conversation. They can earn cult status and provide evocative reference points in everyone's memories. How many times have you struck up a conversation with a complete stranger based on a television programme? Or remembered something from your childhood based on the TV show you followed at the time? Not everyone dreams of national and international stardom, like hosting your own TV show or appearing in a well-respected drama series, but for many the opportunity to contribute to one of – if not the – country's central entertainment provider is a great motivating force.

The industry is a bizarre one, at times apparently divorced from the world it entertains and sometimes depicts. Television is an obsession for those in the industry and it can be difficult to get a word of sense out of those involved on any other subject. For an outsider, new to the industry, it can appear to be a closed industry where everyone knows everyone else and will not give the time of day to innocent newcomers. The difficulties most people experience in getting into the industry do nothing to soften this image – but that difficulty is simply because there isn't enough work to go round. The industry is notorious for lack of security at work and unemployment among qualified personnel. One interviewee for this book noted that more people come out of full-time education looking for work in this area each year than there are people currently employed by the industry.

Having said that, you will find some areas of TV making – technically and geographically – have more vacancies than others. There are skills shortages in some parts of post-production work, while one person I spoke to claimed that the right person with the right skills could find a great career waiting for them in Scotland. The advent of digital TV, cable companies and satellite channels suggests the market place will expand into the future and the viewer won't simply be spoilt for choice; they won't actually be able to make a choice. Sure, there will be a lot of repeats – specialist channels featuring old programmes and so on – but there will also be brand new opportunities and hours more broadcast time to be filled. And in the end TV is a financial equation. For those working on a television programme, whatever artistic or creative aims they have, they must be met within the programme's budget. The overall object of the exercise is to produce a TV programme which a broadcaster wants to buy to show on their network. The only way they will do that is if they believe your programme will attract a significant audience which in turn will attract a number of advertisers to buy the space around the programme, thus financing the TV company. The BBC, supported by licence payers' money, has a different challenge in the programmes it shows, but still must be able to justify the expenditure through the quality and popularity of its output.

> There can be few people who have not dreamed of being on TV at some time or another. Ranks of drama and English students crave their 15 years of fame as a chat show host or starring in their own comedy, although few manage to get on to the screen. However, over the past few years, TV has shown how anyone can be a star. There have been many examples where complete unknowns have been put on screen, hosting programmes simply because their faces fitted. There have been some appalling performers and, indeed, some shows have even enjoyed success because of the amateur appearance of the programme. In addition, the fad for 'fly-on-the-wall' documentaries has made stars out of vets, learner drivers and cruise ship workers. At the time of writing, the quickest way to become a TV celebrity is to invite a documentary maker into your life, sit back and wait.

> The performance and presenting side of TV has always operated in this way. Few presenters actually started out their careers wanting to be presenters – they just happened to be around and able to do the job when it came up. Many presenters are former TV secretaries, spotted on site, while others had already established themselves in a particular field – journalism, scientific writing, radio broadcasting, musical knowledge – which makes them ideal for a particular show. It's worth noting the case of Adam and Joe who secured their own national TV show on Channel 4 through appearing on an 'Open Access' television show with a video they made in their bedroom. One of my friends often appears on television – he's been on *Newsnight*, *Kilroy* and even *All Rise for Julian Clary*. He's got nothing to do with TV but is campaigns officer for a national charity.

Working in television is not, however, limited to appearing on screen. Behind the pictures which appear on your television are a whole host of other jobs. These range from technical work – preparing and broadcasting the programmes – through to the creative side of writing scripts and researching material for TV shows. These roles may appear to be less glamorous but they can be equally fulfilling, creative and exciting.

To get some idea of the different roles, let's imagine we're about to make a drama series.

Pre-production

First off we need a writer to write the script. There are hundreds of aspiring writers, all mad keen to get something – anything – which they've written in development and on screen. Actually there are so many writers out there as soon as we even suggest we're interested in hearing from people with 'never before performed' scripts, we're going to be inundated with thousands of them. We therefore need a team of readers to sift through the scripts and pick out a good one for us to produce.

Having selected a script we then need a production manager and a director who will take charge of all the various elements of the production and ensure the programme gets made on time and within the budget we can spend on the show. Together, these two will locate and co-ordinate everything from the camera crew who will shoot the programme – on film or video – through to post-production facilities where the programme can be edited and prepared for broadcast.

The first thing the production manager needs to do is get the script into a shootable format. They may liaise with the writer and even employ a script editor for this and will certainly take input from the programme's director before the final version is agreed. The director will be responsible for the performances in the drama – the way the production feels and looks. Having established the blueprint for the programme, they can now appoint the production crew which will shoot the show. Among these personnel is the location manager who will travel around for the next few weeks finding suitable locations where the film can be shot. An art director will be appointed to take care of the set and the props needed for the show. Wardrobe staff will be employed to dress the characters and there may be work for set constructors – builders, carpenters, plumbers, plasterers and even gardeners. A lighting designer will design lighting effects and brief the lighting riggers and technical crew on how to light the location for each shooting day.

The production manager will need to contact a casting agent to find the actors for the piece. Auditions may be held or there may be a number of screen tests in which the director will decide which actor he wants to play which character.

Production

TV and film production is all about teamwork and each of these workers will consult each other as they gradually move towards the creation of the show. There will be researchers, assistants and secretarial roles in each area supporting the work. Runners will also be employed to do the menial jobs required to co-ordinate the diverse areas of the production.

The overwhelming characteristic of work in TV drama – and in other areas of television – is of demarcation. There are hundreds of jobs behind a single TV show – many more than you see on the closing credits – and they are all responsible for specific parts of the show. Take the camera crew, for example. This is not simply one person pointing the camera in the right direction and making sure the shot stays in focus, but a group of people each with responsibility for moving one part of the camera. One person will make sure the shot stays in focus, another will make sure the camera moves in the right way to follow the shot, another may be responsible for swivelling the camera for a particular effect. Sound is taken care of separately by engineers who record the action as it happens and ensure sound effects and background noise are also available ready for editing together the final programme.

In the art and design department there may be one person responsible for deciding what props to buy, another for buying and hiring those props – and negotiating the best price. Another will be responsible for the use and maintenance of those articles on set. In a television studio there will be people employed simply to run errands for the director. One assistant on a studio-based TV programme had the job of listening out for errors in what the presenter was saying. On the same programme he was also put in charge of a particularly rowdy studio audience of teenagers.

This division of labour is necessary because there are so many areas where things can go wrong. If one person were left to operate the camera there's a chance that the shot would drift out of focus whenever the camera operator tried to move to a different shot. If everyone concentrates on playing their part correctly the programme should be made with very few hitches. The large number of people required makes drama for television one of the most expensive types of television production. Those involved must know their work inside out and make sure everything goes smoothly. And, if anything does go wrong finding the person responsible is extremely easy.

Shooting can last for weeks and months at diverse locations. Dramas are rarely, if ever, shot in sequence – once at a certain location all those scenes will be recorded, before moving on to the next location and so on. Some scenes may be shot in a studio. During the shoot there will be additional wardrobe and make-up staff on hand to prepare the actors and a mobile catering service to provide refreshments and meals throughout the day.

Post-production

Once shooting is complete, making the programme isn't even half over. There are a whole host of technical processes to go through before the programme can be transmitted. To begin with the editor, together with the director, must take the film and cut it into the correct sequence, creating the final show as originally envisaged. A sound editor will match the sound track, combining what was recorded on location with additional voice-over material and music. There may be other sound effects to be added during the dub – where the programme's sound track is recorded. In some cases the entire sound track for one particular scene may be re-recorded in a sound studio using Foley Artists who provide sound effects to match the action.

The fully assembled programme then goes through a series of technical processes making the picture and sound ready for broadcast. These include the negative cut, picture grading and the sound dub. While all this has been happening a scheduler at the broadcasting company will have identified a suitable time for the show to be broadcast. Leading up to this date publicists will go to work, and trailers will be made to promote the show to viewers. In the weeks before transmission takes place actors and even the director will help to promote the show through interviews with other parts of the media – newspapers, TV and radio.

Current affairs

Now let's suppose we're putting together a studio-based current affairs show. Where previously we were looking for a writer to create our programme, we now need someone to come up with an original idea – or at least an interesting take on an old format – for the show. We may need to employ an entire development team to realize the show. These people will be involved in researching suitable stories, working them up into items for the programme and deciding how these stories should be presented. Again we need a production manager to co-ordinate all aspects of the show. A director or a programme editor will be responsible for the overall content and style of the show as it is broadcast.

Our programme is to be shot in a studio. Shooting here requires the services of set designers, properties managers, lighting and sound engineers, as well as camera operators. TV centres will have their own trained camera operators for this task. The show may contain pre-filmed elements or segments of live outside broadcasts. This means dispatching a technical team – camera crew, sound and lighting engineers – plus a presenter to the location. We may broadcast the show live or pre-record ready for transmission. Either way the director of the show will sit in the gallery, a box room at the back of the studio, watching the pictures produced by each of the cameras in the studio, and decide the mix between them which appears on the public's TV screens.

So, while you may believe the only place for you in TV is in front of the camera, you will find there are a whole host of exciting and fulfilling jobs of which the public remain blissfully unaware. Sometimes these roles are more challenging and exciting than fronting the show itself. Presenters and actors can be very detached from the actual creation of a show, simply performing and having no control of or contribution to the final appearance of the piece at all.

Obsession

In all areas of television work the people involved in producing programmes are obsessed by the media. They will be able to quote details of former television programmes verbatim at you, telling you everything from the broadcast time to the name of the director and camera operator. Listening to two editors discuss a TV programme is like eavesdropping on a conversation in a foreign language. They can spot details which completely pass by the average viewer – mistakes in lip-synching, continuity mistakes where some detail of the picture has changed between two shots intended to be similar. Editors know the grammar of television – how cutting from one shot to another in a specific time will affect the story told to the audience and affect their emotions. Sound engineers will be fiercely critical of every piece of sound mixing they hear – they are automatically attuned to sudden increases or decreases in background noise.

This level of knowledge can only be attained through years of experience and you may feel a bit left out when you first come into the industry. More importantly, you have to face it that if you want to succeed in the industry you need to be as obsessed as everybody else. Can you handle the idea of working in TV all day and then coming home to more television? It's a leisure pursuit for most people but if you're involved in making it you may never be able to switch off in front of the screen again.

The problem with trying to write about getting into television is that just as there are countless jobs there are an infinite number of ways in which you can get into the industry. Moreover, once in the industry your career path may prove extremely haphazard compared with those in more mundane industries.

Make no mistake – it is a harsh industry. There are the back biters, the cynics and those who appear to be riding on a wave of apathy within the industry – getting work simply because they are in the right place at the right time rather than through any great skill on their part.

Perhaps the most bizarre comment I heard from interviewees I spoke to for this book was that the food in television is good. On location, TV production crews have regular breaks throughout the day and dedicated catering teams to feed them. The food is also pretty good in 'on-line' facility houses involved in post-production processes. However, this is a far cry from working in a production office where pressure of work may mean you don't have time to eat during the day. Editors and technicians here spend most of their working days in front of TV screens and equipment in dark editing rooms. While production workers on location may travel thousands of miles for their work, editors and technicians may work for weeks without seeing daylight.

To make matters worse, talk to anyone in television and they won't make a fuss of the media they work in. It's just a job like anything else. If you have a romantic view of working in television, perhaps you should reconsider your career choice. Working in television can destroy your enthusiasm for the media. The work can simply amount to drudgery and clock watching. Can you live with the idea that your interest may just become another working day?

2

Sleeping your way to the top (and other partial myths)

Ask anyone in TV what they used to do in their free time when they were younger and you'll find it had something to do with what they do now. Perhaps they were involved in the theatre – rigging lights, performing, stage managing. Perhaps they were already playing around with video cameras – experimenting with framing shots or trying to edit material with two video recorders linked together. Maybe they were already writing ideas for TV shows. If you are serious about working in television, you should already have a healthy obsession with the box. What you need to do now is channel all that enthusiasm into a plan of attack on the industry.

The industry is receptive to mavericks – to bright young things with great ideas. Television is hungry for innovation and original concepts. There may be many people involved in creating TV but not that many with exciting and ground-breaking ideas. If you don't believe me, take a look at tonight's TV schedule and see how many programmes could truly be described as new.

Armed with a VHS video camera it is possible to find you have a natural flair for camera work and try to sell yourself as a freelance worker regardless of the training you haven't had. You only need to look at the meteoric rise of Chris Evans to see how fame can be taken by those with fashionable ideas, bags of energy and confidence. You may completely hate Evans and Ginger Productions but there's no getting away from the fact that he makes commercial television. By the same token, without constantly adapting the product, there's always a chance that Evans will sink into obscurity as fashion moves on.

Before you start your campaign you should have a clear idea of what precisely you want to do when you get into TV. If you want to be a documentaries director the experience you will need and route your career should take will be completely different to that of a drama producer. In the early days you will probably take whatever menial task is given to you – as long as it's in television. But as time goes by and your experience builds you must be selective about what you do – and even more selective about what you don't do.

Some people in the industry believe there is a divide between 'craft' work in television – camera operating, set building, lighting and so on – and the 'creative' side – directing, producing, presenting. It is difficult to identify these two areas of work precisely – editing for example is a technical process that is also very creative – but in an industry which demands specialist knowledge it is not easy to make an effective switch between one discipline and another. Less strict barriers separate people who work on creating drama programmes, those on documentaries, light entertainment and other genres of show. Again, specialization among producers and other roles for these genres can help a high-flying career, but it is easier to transfer your skills between programme genres than specific jobs. Wherever you start you should have a clear initial interest in a specific kind of programme and what you'd like to do on that programme – this will focus your efforts in the early years and help people in positions of power to relate to you and give you the right breaks.

Three routes

In spite of the multiple ways into the industry, I've identified three main routes, as follows.

1. You have a contact in the industry already. This could be anyone in any position in the industry at all. It could be the next-door neighbour of a distant relative who does a bit of research for television from time to time. Phone them up and tell them what

you want to do. Get their advice and see if they know of any openings or other people to whom you should speak. Many people believe that getting anywhere in television means sycophantically ingratiating yourself with anyone who can give you what you want. This is only partially true. Using contacts is essentially getting a leg up into the industry – cutting a corner, if you like – by telling people who you are and what you want to do without having to get a job in the industry first. The industry relies on recommendations – no one will put a good word in for someone who can't do the job. It'll be no surprise then, that if you do get into the industry by personal contact and can't pull your weight or do the job you will not survive five minutes.

2. Send your CV off to as many production or post-production companies as you can find. Go to the local reference library and find *The White Book* or *Kemp's Directory*. This will tell you which companies are involved in which areas of television production and where to send your CV. A golden tip is to keep sending off your CV to the same companies every three or four months. This is because when they receive a CV it goes on the top of the pile: the CV belongs to someone who's looking for work now and if the company needs an extra pair of hands at short notice there's more likelihood that the person on top of the pile will be available.

3. The training route usually applies to the more technically based disciplines and over-subscription is notorious. The BBC take on about half a dozen students each year as production trainees, and a similar number as sound engineers and camera operators. This leaves over 9,980 disappointed applicants. The BBC has always given more people a start in television through unofficial training than through official courses. Research work, secretarial jobs and work experience of every kind provides much easier access for someone starting out in TV than trying to compete through the application form. The British Film School runs courses in many areas of production although it is interesting to note that successful applicants here have usually spent some time working in the industry already – thus proving their dedication to the medium.

Right skills, right time

No matter which of these three routes you take, you'll find that getting that first job is a matter of being able to offer the right skills to the right person at the right time. Those skills may be the ability to work a video camera or to cut a film. They may equally be the ability to organize a busy office and make a good cup of tea, or to be able to rabbit on in front of a camera about nothing in particular for a specific length of time.

Take the example of the presenter who first worked introducing videos on a Europe-wide pop music channel. He'd been involved in music for quite a while and was working with a pop group on tour around the world. With a performance background – acting classes as a child, singing lessons and so on – he was already fairly outgoing and confident in front of an audience. Whenever the cameras arrived to film the band he'd always be put forward as spokesman for the group. A friend of his had recently been turned down for work as a video jockey and the friend suggested he should have a go. With first-hand knowledge of music and natural performance skills, he got the job. On the one hand he had the right skills, while on the other he knew someone who knew of an opportunity.

Both skills and knowledge lay behind another presenter's big break, although the story here appears to go against the grain. With extensive training and background in journalism this individual had not even considered the possibility of working in television, preferring the reporting challenges of radio and print. However, she applied for a journalist presenter job advertised in the pages of the *Guardian* – and was appointed. So, despite what everyone says, applying to ads in the paper can actually work.

Screen tests, show reels and showing off

In both of these examples, the presenters were put through their paces with a 'screen test' to see how they would appear on television. Anyone who does a screen test feels the same nerves as for any other job interview, but in reality the director or producer carrying out the test is on your side. They will give you the opportunity to see what you can do rather than try to catch you out. You may be asked to prepare a presentation which they will film from a variety of angles. Alternatively, you may be given three things to do – talk about a video which is playing out, remind viewers of a phone-in competition and lead into the next item. While this is happening the director may suddenly throw a spanner in the works – the next item isn't happening and you have to fill in for another 60 seconds. . . It doesn't matter if you make a complete mess of this – it will give the director an idea of what you can do in front of the camera.

It may be useful to have your own 'show reel' prepared so TV companies can see what you can do. If you do make your own show reel the best thing to do is make it about something. Don't just stand in front of the camera saying who you are and what you do. Talk about something, present a story, show you can research and put together an informative package. The final product does not need to be broadcast quality but evidence of televisual awareness will have far greater impact than just your own ego.

The majority of presenters started out in TV doing something completely different. Secretaries, researchers and even technicians have been suddenly 'discovered'. In all cases these people had one thing in common – they already knew how television worked and what was required from them.

If you have had no contact with the industry and are a complete newcomer you must immerse yourself in the media as much as possible now. Read the industry press on a regular basis. Study the media pages of the national press and form your own ideas on the current state of TV. Make yourself familiar with the world of your chosen career. Get to know the names of important people in TV companies – get to understand job titles – what people do and how they contribute. You might read about a new TV programme about to go into production – if so, send your CV off to the producer and see if they can offer you work experience on the programme. When your break comes – if a producer or director decides to interview you for a possible position – make sure you impress them with your knowledge and enthusiasm.

In some respects the industry operates a kind of apprenticeship structure. Those already in the industry are happy to talk and advise on the way things are done and to pass on their own wisdom to the next generation. This is particularly prevalent in the trade disciplines. However, even among the creative side there are opportunities for casual mentorships.

Starting out

For most people, the first role they have in a TV company is as a runner or a researcher. Runners are employed throughout the industry – in production and post-production. As the name suggests, the runner dashes around all over the place completing whatever errands need doing. On location the runner forms an important communication link between the various parts of the production unit. They may be responsible for fetching and carrying equipment or simply helping to co-ordinate the shoot. In post-production, tasks may include fetching and carrying tapes from one production facility to another or transferring tapes between formats. In both situations one of the runner's most important duties will be to make tea for everyone.

Researchers are employed across different kinds of programmes. They are obviously needed for research on consumer programmes – finding stories from members of the public about washing machines that don't wash and finding people who will speak about their experience for the show. Some drama programmes also employ researchers to help give the show authenticity. They are sent out to find real-life stories which can be used to influence the show or research certain time periods for the design and art departments. It should be noted that on some programmes research is not a menial job. Researchers for documentaries, for example, are integral since the material they find will make up the central stories told within the programme. For this reason there are some senior, highly skilled researchers in the industry.

Another side of research is script reading. The BBC still receives scripts from budding writers every week and needs readers to sift through and search out new ideas. One of the first jobs I was offered was script reading for a screenplay competition – a curious occurrence given that appreciating what makes a good programme only really comes with experience. At the same time, as long as you have a clear idea of what you think makes good television and can explain the difference between good and bad drama it can be a good way in. Script readers often take this route into drama production roles – working on the script they themselves have selected.

Whatever you end up doing it is unlikely that you will be paid for your first job in television. What you will get, however, is the opportunity to learn first hand how TV works. Putting together a show is extremely complicated and getting to know who does what and how each individual relates to another is a task in itself. It is possible to learn this from media courses or film school, but it is unlikely that you will be given a job to do in the industry without a practical working knowledge of how those structures work, and the only way to get that is by observing it at first hand.

One editor I spoke to started work experience at a post-production office in the week when everyone else in the company was away working in a different studio. He was left to manage the phones and keep the rooms tidy. On another occasion, having been with the company for over 6 months, they were given 30 hours of film to synchronize with a sound track. They were shown how to do this operation once and then left to complete the entire job. The first job can seem like being thrown in at the deep end, but there are usually people around willing to help with problems and to coach newcomers.

Training up

Training courses do not guarantee a job in the industry. Moreover, a course with such little focus as 'a media course' is unlikely to cut any ice whatsoever within the industry. EVERYONE'S done a media course of some description. A vocational course – or at least one which offers real skills – may give you more standing, simply because you will have had some experience of creating television even if it wasn't actually with a real television company.

A freelance, working as a camera assistant, told me he had taken a post-graduate film course having completed a first degree in science. The course he took certainly introduced him to the kind of equipment used in the production of programmes and gave him the chance the work on his own ideas and therefore build up some experience of what might happen in the real world. Problems which he encountered – lack of continuity between shots, sound problems and so on – were all elements which have to be considered in the real world. However, having completed the course, he then endured two years of poverty before building enough of a reputation to be able to survive as a freelance camera assistant.

Another trainee I spoke to had studied film editing at the British Film School, spending practically all of his time on the course cutting together programmes developed by other people at the school. He was fully versed in documentaries and dramas, and worked with dedication on both. The film school is aimed at producing skilled people ready for the industry and certainly students gain an amount of kudos with the school and opportunities to network with people in the industry. On leaving the school the trainee secured a couple of documentary programmes to work on, however in the long term he too experienced financial hardship through lack of work. He simply was not well enough known to be able to generate continual work.

Another training course is FT2 – Freelance Training for Film and Television. This course is supported by the industry itself through a levy system. Production companies take on students from the course to work in various roles in television. Students work in all areas of television production – regardless of the role they intend to pursue for a living. Alongside their placements they will take some classroom-based study in their chosen area – camera operation, editing, production management and so on. At the end of two years, if nothing else, the students have an impressive CV covering an array of work in diverse productions.

The course is extremely draining and unsurprisingly there's a probationary period at the beginning during which students can reflect on whether this is really what they want to do. One FT2 student told me that the hours demanded by the course were eventually too much – he became so wrapped up in what he was doing and so tired out he was run over on his way to work. While the course unquestionably offers a great insight into the industry, students are not given any special treatment by the people they are working with. There are no concessions because the FT2 student is still getting to learn the ropes. In some cases students have simply got in the way of otherwise efficient production companies.

While the student above left the course following his untimely meeting with an automobile, he did not leave the industry altogether. In some respects FT2 did its job. He took a contract with one of the programmes he was working on at the time, thus moving seamlessly from student to professional worker in one go.

3

How to win jobs and influence programmes

There is no career structure in television. The only progression you will experience will be within your first few years of working – the progression from being an unpaid runner, researcher or assistant, to becoming a paid, recognized television employee. You might be able to start as a researcher and slowly work your way up through positions of responsibility to your goal of producer – but only if that's the direction you want to go in and you actively pursue that path. Some people don't want any more responsibility – they just like being a researcher and will stay in that job for their entire career. Once you have reached your goal – as producer, location manager or whatever – it will be up to you to find new projects to get involved with, and to negotiate your own terms and conditions of employment.

The industry is populated by freelances. The BBC and other TV production companies may offer some long-term contracts, but the trend is increasingly for short-term work. Some people employed by companies on long-running programmes have found themselves doing over 12 months' work, but only through contracts of 10 weeks or less. In other words, as soon as one contract has expired terms need to be re-negotiated. A short-term contract means your employer does not have to support your pension scheme, or provide holiday or sick pay, although the BBC will give the latter two benefits after three months' continuous work. The main attraction of short-term contracts is that the company can drop you as soon as their financial position changes or they think they can do without you.

Wherever you end up working you'll find you're faced with irregular, long hours and hard work. It's not even particularly interesting work half the time. Research and development discussions may go on for hours into the night and resolve to do nothing new. A location shoot for a drama may take for ever – extending filming time into the night for a shot which ends up on the cutting-room floor. Getting technical equipment to do precisely what it is meant to do can result in technicians working through to the small hours of the morning.

Attitudes towards the hours appear to vary throughout the industry, but in fact everyone accepts them as par for the course.

The following snapshots are designed to give you an insight into working in the industry. On the one hand they illustrate a few particular roles which might interest you, but on the other hand they provide an insight into areas of TV work. Presenting, for example, will give you an idea of what it is like to perform in front of the cameras. Location management is a good way of viewing outside location shooting and production work. The snapshots also feature technical and office-based work which again will give you a general feel for this area.

SNAPSHOT OF WORKING LIFE – THE PRESENTER

Anyone can be a presenter – so one presenter told me. Anyone can do it. You just need the ability to talk to the camera and the confidence to keep talking no matter what happens. The trick is getting the opportunity to do it.

From the outside, the job of television presenter looks easy, glamorous and incredibly good fun. Where else can you leap around in front of a camera, take part in all manner of exciting activities, interview the rich and famous and get paid for it? Whether you're on *Top of the Pops* or a Saturday morning kids' show, everyone knows your name, everyone thinks you're great and everyone wants to be you.

The fact is, the typical day of your average television presenter is spent sitting at home wondering whether your house will be repossessed and panicking that you'll never work again. Having been thrust into the limelight once it's incredibly disheartening to feel no one needs your skills again. A presenter might work for a total of three months a year, with jobs dotted around in very intensive blocks of recording. That leaves nine other months of wandering around doing nothing. The show might be on television – you might be a celebrity – but what the hell do you do with the spare days???

For some reason presenting does pay a lot of money. The work isn't terribly hard – not as hard work as being a builder or a professional decorator – which leaves even some presenters mystified as to why they earn so much money. But then, having received thousands of pounds for one half-hour show you may spend the next 18 months surviving on £60 earned for one quick advertisement voice-over recording. Being able to deal with the highs and the incredible lows of the business – reconciling the TV persona and the private life – is possibly the biggest problem for presenters. Self-belief and dedication are extremely important if you are to pursue a career in this area without having a nervous breakdown or resorting to serious drug abuse.

There are many different kinds of presenters. Some may be journalists – newscasters perhaps, or even on-the-spot reporters presenting news story segments for specific programmes. Some will work as programme researchers and may be involved with the development of programmes – even to the point of producing the entire show through their own production company. At the other end of the scale there are the professional presenters who only present. These are usually the high-flying celebrity presenters – game show hosts, event hosts and so on – who turn up on the day and read whatever's on the autocue in front of them as if the words had just popped into their heads.

Successful presenters cultivate an identity which makes them recognizable to the public and aligns them to particular types of programmes. They may trade purely on their personality – it does not have to be a particularly sophisticated or attractive personality, but one which the public has learned to expect from that individual. Alternatively presenters will specialize in children's programmes, music programmes, factual or documentaries. The subject will have some connection to that presenter – a professional scientist could end up presenting a technical show for example. For those starting out in this area you should think about what you can talk about – what subjects would suit you for presentation work. You will find it much easier to start out on a subject with which you are familiar.

Whatever kind of presenter you are you will need certain specific presentation skills. Whether recording in a studio or live broadcasting, the presenter must be able to communicate with the television audience, speak to time and ensure the programme holds together. One presenter claimed talking to the camera was a matter of speaking to just one individual – regardless of the millions glued to the programme. Another simply found he could talk naturally to the camera without even thinking about who was watching.

During a programme the presenter is likely to be dealing with two or three events at once. He may be reciting lines to the camera, getting ready to introduce another item and keeping track of how much longer the programme has to run. In the midst of all this, if there are any technical hitches, it is up to the presenter to keep things moving and coherent for the viewer.

A lot of the time this means presenters are working on adrenalin. Adrenalin is produced by your body at times of stress and excitement to give you the energy and awareness to adapt to whatever happens around you. It's an extremely effective way of working and incredibly exhilarating at the time, but it is also exhausting. Therefore, as soon

How to win jobs and influence programmes 25

as the shooting is over, the presenter comes down from this peak of adrenalin and is usually asleep within minutes.

Take the typical recording day for a presenter of a television series. Development and planning meetings will have taken place for a series of six to eight shows over a period of about ten days. These meetings will discuss the script, content, technical and props requirements for each show. The presenter will be involved in this, providing script advice and ensuring all elements of their performance have been considered.

Immediately following those meetings, the entire series will be shot in one block of six or seven days in a studio at a television centre. On these days the presenter gets up at 6, gets to the studio at 7.30, goes through make-up and arrives on the studio floor by 9am. Filming then begins, and apart from lunch and tea breaks, continues solidly until 6.30pm. When performing to camera adrenalin and energy levels are high. As soon as the camera comes off, the energy level comes down. One presenter explained that whenever the cameras moved away from him he'd cat-nap under the presenter's desk, simply because he needed all the energy he could get for the pieces which involved him.

At 6.30pm you go back to the hotel room, unable to communicate with anyone else because your head is still full of today's shooting and worrying about what will happen tomorrow. A live TV show requires even more energy as a cock-up here will instantly be broadcast to the nation. Recording an entire series may result in a fortnight of intensive work, day in day out. A weekly live TV show over a number of months can be even more tiring. In both cases working with this intensity can be extremely disorientating.

Of course, some shows do not demand a high-octane, rapid-fire approach. A laid-back, daytime programme for example may be stressful, but because of the slower pace and style it is less likely to burn you out before you reach 35.

A good career in TV presenting may cover only two or three programmes – if successful programmes are recommissioned and they still want to use you they can go on for years. Build a strong enough reputation in one role and it is likely that a producer will seek you out for another project they are doing. Make a mess of a programme and you've had it.

SNAPSHOT OF WORKING LIFE –
THE LOCATION MANAGER

Employed principally on drama programmes, location managers can earn substantial amounts of money in short periods of time. However, this money sometimes appears poor compensation for one of the most stressful jobs in the area of programme production. Location management can seem little short of miracle working. The main task is to find suitable locations for filming to take place – a drama can require many different scenes – interiors of particular houses, exterior shots in woodlands, housing estates and so on. Having made arrangements with the owner(s) of each location so they can use it for filming on the days required, the location manager is then responsible for everything that happens on site when the rest of the production crew turn up.

All this must be done to a strict time scale – the shooting schedule will already state when specific locations will be used – and to a strict budget. The location budget covers payments to the owners for the inconvenience of having a camera crew marauding over their property all day and for additional building or location dressing required for the shoot. Having at last found the correct house for one programme, one location manager then had to spend an extra few thousand pounds building a garden path and a shed in the back garden, as required by the script. This building also had to be removed and the garden returned to its previous state when shooting was complete. Going over budget, or failing to have a location ready when required, will result in the programme losing money. This is not good news for the production company and especially not good news for the career of the location manager.

Work begins at the early stages of production. With six to eight weeks to go before shooting takes place the location manager will be appointed by the programme's producer and brought in to discuss the locations required with the director, producer and designer. A simple request such as 'a comprehensive school corridor' may suddenly become extremely difficult to find if the designer has specific demands to be met or the script requires a specific number of entrances and exits. The manager will be given a timetable of when shooting will start and when these locations will be required. There follows a period of travelling around in search of places which match these demands.

This part of the job is the most pleasant – finding new places, talking to the owners and discovering the history of buildings. Local councils and heritage organizations are now very enthusiastic to get their locations featured on the small screen. This makes the job of finding locations easier, but makes them more expensive as such organizations are now getting wise to the remuneration possible through this work. The location manager takes photos and video footage of each location to give an overall impression of the place for the designer and director. However, as the starting date for shooting draws nearer, there are always one or two locations which prove elusive, causing sleepless nights, more frantic travelling between locations and tactical discussions with the director and designer to persuade them to accept the location already found.

Once the location has been agreed the manager has to set the location up. This involves contacting everyone around the location to notify them when filming will be taking place. The local police need to be notified – and sometimes even nearby airports if pyrotechnics are involved. The manager has to find the best route for the crew to reach the location – bearing in mind this can include a fleet of articulated lorries carrying equipment. Maps are drawn up and distributed. If anyone gets lost on the way, it's the location manager's fault.

On the day of recording, the location manager is the first person to arrive and the last to leave the site. He's there to supervise the parking of the crew's vehicles – cars and lorries – and to make sure everyone knows where they're going. Preparation is everything: if you've done your homework you'll already be aware of the problems that could arise during the shoot. As soon as any of these problems do arise, you will be expected to solve them instantly.

Problems can include anything from dealing with members of the public who are getting in the way of the recording to negotiating new arrangements with the property owners if the director decides to do something different. The location manager will also be expected to handle any complaints from the locals while the film crew are working.

Once everyone has packed up and gone home, the location manager has to make sure everything is returned to the condition in which it was found before shooting began. He'll have to clean and replace damaged items, go around the site and throw away any rubbish – especially the plastic beakers from the catering truck – and finally clean the toilets.

By the time he's done that it will probably be about 2am. There'll be a few hours to go home and sleep – but not that many. The shooting schedule means next day the entire crew will turn up at a new location and the location manager will be up at 5am, travelling to get there before anyone else arrives.

These long and stressful hours can continue from four to eight weeks non stop. Even before shooting begins he will be at the producer's beck and call – a mobile phone call away from another production team member with another problem. And that's why, on a weekly basis, location managers command some of the highest fees in the industry. It is possible to work for four months and then take the next four months off. But boy, do you need that holiday.

SNAPSHOT OF WORKING LIFE – CAMERA ASSISTANT AND LIGHTING RIGGER

Technical work can appear to be simply the application of a skill to the television media and in some cases this is true. A lighting rigger is going to spend time carrying around cable and lights whether he's working in the theatre or on location. A sound recordist for a film is doing the same job as someone recording material for a radio programme – there may be differences in the kind of material gathered and in the quality of sound required – but essentially it's the same job. Similarly, operating a camera will require the same skills whether you're working on film, television drama or pop videos. There may be different shots to get and you may be dealing with different recording formats, but at the end of the day it's about getting the right shot through the lens.

Sometimes 'jobsworth' appears to prevail. One television worker involved in location work explained the difference in attitude which appeared to exist between the technical and craft disciplines and the more creative employees: If recording a shot starts to go over the amount of time allotted to filming, the 'creative' people – the director and producer – will encourage team spirit and try to get everyone working together to get this great shot. The technical crew, meanwhile, will start muttering about being paid overtime. In fact, they are probably as committed to getting the shot right as anyone else – but it's not the done thing to admit to that.

At the end of the day, the job of both the camera assistant and the lighting rigger is to do whatever is necessary to realize the ideas of the director. If the director wants a shot which begins in close-up then slowly moves out to a more encompassing view, the camera crew must work together in order to do that. There may be difficulties in getting that shot – the light may be unsuitable, it may be difficult to move the camera in the right way given the surroundings in which they are shooting – but it's up to them to solve those problems and get the shot.

Similarly, the director might want specific lighting effects for atmospheric conditions or to denote the mood of the piece. The lighting designer will take this into consideration when deciding what lights to put where, but it is up to the rigger to ensure these lights are positioned correctly, will operate safely and produce that effect.

The lighting crew will be among the first to arrive on set – whether it be on location or in a studio. On location it is likely that a team of scaffolders will have already erected the structure on which the lights will be hung. It is then a matter of hanging the lights, plugging them in and making sure they're all pointing in the right direction. In the TV studio there will already be lights on the rigging in the ceiling. These will need focusing according to the lighting designer's plan.

Just as in the theatre, the lights must be rigged and focused before any of the set goes up. In the studio there may be an entire set that has to be constructed before the programme can be recorded. Trying to put lights up around that is impossible.

Lighting can be heavy work. There are all sorts of heavy pieces of equipment to lug around, and given location work can involve muddy fields and terrible weather it may not be much fun or exactly inspiring work. With a bit of luck, rigging will be completed fairly quickly and the entire lighting crew can go off down the pub for lunch before returning in the afternoon to either complete the work, or to take the equipment down and put it away.

Some jobs, however, do offer unique challenges. One rigger I spoke to worked on a large outdoor event which was to be broadcast live. Seconds before the show went on air one of the major lights failed, putting an extra load of electricity through another circuit. The show went ahead with a lighting rig that was constantly in danger of overheating and closing down. It's an exciting position to be in and can be very nerve-racking, using your technical knowledge and skills to react and troubleshoot problems immediately.

Lighting systems and control equipment have become far more sophisticated over the last few years, and lighting teams need to know precisely what kind of equipment they can use in order to get the desired effect. Alongside this knowledge, a resilient constitution will also help you survive the rigours of a location job.

The difficulty of operating a TV camera – and thus the skills and training you require to be a TV camera operator today – depends on the type of equipment and the format being used. In a BBC studio, broadcast camera people will have undergone official training to get to know the equipment and how to work on a programme. During a recording or broadcast, the cameras will be directed by the show's director communicating to them through headphone and microphone links. If you ever get a glimpse of a studio camera, you'll see it's a huge thing with all kinds of controls to aid manoeuvrability. On other formats cameras are very much smaller and can be moved around by one or two people. Digital video (DV) cameras even offer broadcast quality recording from a hand-held camera.

For pre-recorded material – documentaries, pop videos, advertisements or drama – the director will decide what kind of format to shoot on, whether video or film. Different kinds of formats will require camera operators and assistants to do different tasks. In general, assistants have to look after the equipment, keep it in good, clean working order and dash around supplying the camera operator with everything he wants. The assistant may act as clapper loader – on hand to load the camera with more film stock or video tape when the current one runs out and to mark the 'clapper' – the board shown in front of the camera before a scene is shot marking the shot number and the name of the production.

Loading film must be done in compete darkness which usually entails fumbling around inside a black bag doing everything by touch. One camera assistant pointed out that you have to be good at this because there are occasions when you're under pressure to get it done very quickly. He was working on a documentary and found himself in the middle of a riot trying to load film so the camera operator could record the events as they happened around them.

As a focus puller, your job is to ensure the picture always stays in focus no matter where the camera is pointing. Since you can't actually see through the lens the job is more to do with mathematics than making adjustments according to the image. Focus pullers must know how far away the subject is from the camera lens and adjust the focus correctly. Clearly a moving subject presents additional challenges.

No matter what format is used, camera operators need a lot of technical knowledge. They need to assess lighting conditions and the speed of action taking place so they can adjust the camera accordingly. Knowing the theory is all very well, but the job can only be done through experience – shooting material and seeing how it comes out.

The ascent to chief camera operator is a slow process of working your way round the equipment, the various roles of the camera assistant and understanding how each one affects the final piece of film. No matter how good you are it's likely to be ten years before you get to be the chief camera operator.

On the way, however, you will work in a wide variety of situations, and the opportunity for travel is high. An assistant camera operator can work on pop videos, advertisements, dramas or documentaries. In general the pay is fairly good but the bonuses – free travel, hospitality and so on – are very attractive. Filming a pop video on location can result in all the excesses you would expect from a rock-and-roll lifestyle.

Drugs of one kind or another are commonplace in this part of the industry. They are available and accepted. A lighting rigger commented that a taste for strong European lager was also definitely a plus for working in this area.

SNAPSHOT OF WORKING LIFE – THE (ASSISTANT) EDITOR

When a programme has been recorded, the director brings all the raw material to a cutting room. It is here that the editor will shape the final programme, selecting the important scenes and dropping material that doesn't come up to scratch or isn't required. A busy cutting room might handle several programmes at once, requiring the careful management of hundreds of video tapes or film reels to ensure the right footage appears in the right programme.

The final shape of the programme is determined by the director and the editor. In most cases the director will have been involved in the programme from the start – carrying out research and directing the actual recording – and so will have a very clear idea of what the programme needs to say and how it should say it. The editor provides a useful objective viewpoint of the material and is able to highlight areas which are unclear. The editor will also suggest different ways of presenting the material in the programme.

Editing itself can be done on film or video – according to the format it has been shot on and to the editor's preference. Often in TV, editing is done on computer editing equipment. The raw material – or rushes – is played into the computer (digitized) and the editor can then select any part of that material to work on in any order. This is known as the off-line edit. The computer produces the details of this edit – what footage has been used and how long for – and this is taken together with the original filmed material to an on-line edit where the programme is assembled at broadcast quality in picture. The sound track is added in a separate process known as the dub.

With so many different kinds of video format in use and the requirement to transfer all the footage for the programme into the computer before any editing can take place, editors and assistant editors can find much of their time taken up with transferring material from one kind of tape to another. Material may come in on DV but must then be transferred to beta tapes for the off-line and on-line edit and to VHS so the directors can view what they've shot. Rushes may also be transferred to audio tape for transcription purposes.

Editing itself is a collaborative process between editor and director, and every working relationship will be different according to the experience of each and the material concerned. Programmes must fit precisely the length of time allocated to them and this can come down to editing out a few frames of action here and there. At the same time a successful edit may only be a few frames different from an unsatisfying one. It's a matter of developing a sense of timing – again, something which will only come through experience. As the programme is assembled, there will be a viewing with the executive producer to ensure the show is heading in the right direction. The executive producer is responsible for the overall standard of the show and may demand some alterations.

As completion draws near the director and editor will work on any necessary voice-over script which will be recorded separately and added to the programme later. The whole process for a half-hour show can take anything up to five weeks to complete – rewarding work but very time consuming. Technical difficulties – machines breaking down or not talking to each other or mis-recording material – can result in long and very frustrating working hours.

Full-time programme editors are employed by production companies on a freelance basis. Some have already invested in thousands of pounds worth of editing equipment and will include the hire of that equipment in any deal they strike with the production company. Surviving as a freelance editor depends on building a good reputation within the industry for your work.

Assistant editors may find themselves doing a whole host of different jobs towards managing the post-production process on a programme. One assistant, working on a long-running documentary series, explained there were several directors shooting material on location and overseeing the editing of shows. This meant the cutting room had to keep track of the material as it came in. Rushes had to be logged so everyone knew what material was there and once directors had decided what they wanted to use in their programmes, the assistant had to be able to find all the rushes relating to each specific story. A large amount of the assistant's time is therefore taken up either with logging rushes or transferring the rushes on to other formats. The assistant editor is something of a dying breed.

Many of these tasks are now carried out by production assistants or by the editors themselves.

Managing the flow of material to and from the camera crews, to the cutting room and to the on-line edit can be a logistical nightmare for post-production workers. The camera crew must have enough stock to continue recording and record material in such a way that will not produce problems later on in the edit – whether through poor sound levels or using the wrong format. There's always the chance that a tape will go astray somewhere or someone will record the wrong thing. With so many responsibilities, the assistant editor, and other post-production workers in this area, must be able to work tactfully with everyone else, be aware of their deadlines and able to prioritize effectively, making sure everything is done according to schedule.

4

The future presentation

The future of television appears chaotic and confusing. The heralded dawn of digital television, of hundreds and thousands of channels providing unlimited choice for viewers, is regarded with relish by some, with dismay and fear by others. Diverse opinions begin at senior level with television company directors disputing whether increased choice will push up the standards of TV programmes or drive them down into an abyss of mediocrity and repeats. Opinion remains split among workers at ground level – will there be more opportunities for editors, cameramen, location managers – or will there be less money to support their work?

The continual reshaping of the BBC, devolving programme making to independent companies, plus the expansion of the television market – Channel 5 already offers another terrestrial channel – has spawned an incredible number of independent television production companies. Some of these have been created to produce one programme only for one particular broadcaster. Others produce a range of programmes for different networks. They may not even serve terrestrial channels, finding instead a lucrative market on satellite or cable broadcasters. Most companies are dedicated to a particular genre of programme making. They are specialists in producing documentaries, comedy shows or light entertainment programmes. As such they will attract the best people with those kind of ideas and be able to convince programme commissioners at the broadcasting companies that they are able to produce high quality programmes in this area.

Broadcasters often collaborate with production companies in the creation of a programme or film. They may share resources, finance and ultimately any revenue the show generates. These alliances can produce interesting working situations: you may be employed by an independent production company using BBC facilities in order to produce a programme which will not receive its premiere on BBC TV.

Independents' day

In some cases production companies have appeared when producers and performers have decided to make the break and set up their own organization to produce the programme they were involved in for the BBC. Such companies may take the freelance staff working on those programmes with them into the new independent company. One assistant editor who followed the programme he was working on from within the BBC to the independent sector explains that the move had a mix of good and bad effects. Within the BBC he'd been working on only one programme and there was little opportunity to meet other people within the company and get them interested in what he could do.

The independent company was a smaller organization. He had more contact with the editors working on the programmes and so could establish himself with them, ensuring that if a job turned up and those editors required an assistant he'd be first on their list. However, the size of the company also meant that his workload increased dramatically. He found himself responsible for areas of production which were previously taken care of elsewhere in the BBC. Hours and stress levels increased, but so too did his experience and knowledge in putting together a programme. Given the amount of work which was coming in, the independent company was able to offer him editing work far earlier than would have been possible through the BBC. This alone means he is already well on the way to building enough experience and contacts to become a fully-fledged freelance editor. While being a good thing for his career, it's completely destroyed his social life: adrenalin keeps him working hard in the cutting rooms until late at night, when everyone else is down the pub. As soon as he gets home the adrenalin stops and he spends most of his time there asleep.

A large number of production companies have been set up by performers, presenters or producers who have already had success within the BBC. Not only do they have experience in creating programmes, but they also have the status and knowledge to be able to sell programmes to the broadcasters. While the financial risk involved in establishing your own company is great, there are great rewards – both financial and artistic – as you gain more control over your own output on television.

No doubt the number of independent television companies will continue to grow in the future and this has to be good news for the newcomer to the industry. Each company offers more opportunities for experience and as companies seek to find the most lucrative niche market for their products, you should be able to target the production company most suited to your own interests and skills in television.

Some in the industry regard the proliferation of independent companies and the slow demise of the BBC as a stable institution for television making as a very positive force. Producers have more control over the programmes they make, cut free of the bureaucracy which used to accompany working for the BBC. At the same time, however, this movement has all but destroyed the possibility for a clear career path. One person I spoke to had worked in the BBC for 17 years – rising from researcher to location manager to producer. He explained that while the jobs he had done may be of use for this book his overall career experience was now completely out of date and would be of no use to newcomers to the industry. No one can expect the BBC to give them a straightforward career path or to develop them in a predictable fashion. Even here there are short-term contracts and the constant threat of redundancy.

Zeros and ones

Digital television will expand the number of television channels viewers can watch at any one time. It will not increase the number of viewers and it certainly will not increase the number of people who can put money into television. It will not increase the number of advertisers and will do nothing to affect the licence fee which goes to support the BBC. The result will be the same amount of money spread over more programmes – therefore less money available for each production.

As mentioned above, presenters at the moment are paid large amounts of money for what they do. Moreover, it is relatively easy to achieve celebrity status and increase your fee since you're appearing on one of only five terrestrial channels. Expand that number and already you will have to work harder and appear on more channels in order to gain celebrity status. If digital television really does bring TV to the masses, even opening community television channels, it could be that appearing on television is no longer viewed with the same awe and reverence currently bestowed upon it. Anyone can do the job – and everyone will have the opportunity to do it. With this realization the amount of money paid to presenters will fall.

Workers in the production and post-production side of television have already experienced the squeeze on financial resources as companies strive to increase their profit margins without compromising the television product. One location manager said he'd have to get out of the profession soon because the shooting schedules were getting ridiculously tight. Production companies are trying to cut costs wherever they can – and since drama productions cost around £15,000 per day to shoot, reducing that time by one or two days can really make a big difference. For workers on location, however, this immediately hikes up the pressure to get it right first time.

Start juggling now

In order to cope with the number of different jobs and the amount of work within the industry, employees are increasingly expected to be multiskilled – to be fully competent in two or three areas of television production rather than just one. Unsurprisingly for an industry where demarcation has always been important, the drive towards multiskilling is meeting with some resistance.

There are many examples of multiskilling. A presenter working on a consumer programme explained that shooting a report for a magazine programme used to mean taking a camera operator, a sound recordist and director on location to get the material. They would already have done their research, would know what the reporter needed to say to the camera at which locations and what information would be given during each interview. While the camera operator and sound recordist took care of the sound and picture, the director would make sure the right shots were collected and that the reporter's performance was as required for the item.

Nowadays, it is more usual for the director to shoot all the footage himself, taking care of sound and lighting while the reporter carries out the interview. The two-person operation may save money at this stage of production, but it can lead to problems further down the line. An editor explained to me that the chief problem with directors shooting their own material was that the quality of material falls, making it extremely difficult to edit into a coherent package. Directors might have a good eye for framing a shot – although still inferior to someone with years of experience behind the lens – but they are less proficient with sound recording. Without the right material recorded at the right quality it can be extremely difficult to edit the material together without sudden changes in sound or jumps in continuity.

In some areas multiskilling has been technology led. With DV (digital video) cameras, anyone can point a camera at an event and record broadcast quality footage – that is to say, the picture quality will be good enough even if framing the picture is not. This has meant that many programme researchers, who previously spent days tied to a desk and telephone finding people to appear on television shows, can now go out and record those people themselves. DV cameras have certainly made 'fly-on-the-wall' documentaries much easier to produce.

Multiskilling is bad news for newcomers to the industry because it is effectively ripping out all the assistant roles. Camera operators no longer need assistants to look after their equipment and help them set up for shooting. Editors can do their own transfers and may be expected to do a full broadcast quality sound mix, whereas previously this would have been left to a dubbing mixer. Producers can instantly cut the overall cost of their production by avoiding the expense of employing their own assistant, delegating work directly to other production managers and secretarial workers.

These assistant positions used to be ideal stamping grounds for people to learn the business and gain experience in programme making. They'd observe how programmes were put together and learn techniques as they were used on various programmes. It is difficult to see how these kinds of opportunities will be available in the future where production companies are run on a lean basis and everyone they take on is expected to pull more than their own weight as soon as they are employed.

Digital television may open up the media for more people to work in, but it does not guarantee a career in the industry and certainly does not guarantee any standard of broadcast quality. Sure, it may be possible to put together your own show and put it out on the community channel, and you may get high praise for your ingenuity and originality, but making an impact on the professional industry is going to get harder. Successful workers will be those who can take more responsibility earlier in their careers. There will be no neutral ground for making mistakes and learning the trade.

Getting into TV will still be easier if you've got good contacts in the industry. However, the need to make an impact on whoever you work for will be far greater. Training could ultimately be the preserve of those with the financial backing to afford it. Similarly, it may only be by paying your own way and working for nothing that you can get the work experience and skills you need to do the job properly.

5

What's on the other side?

Getting into television requires a blend of skill and luck. Staying in television is a little easier.

One editor told me that working in television did not require you to be particularly ruthless, but you had to love it completely. There are so many things to put you off – people, working practices, even the types of programmes you end up working on – that without a basic love of the box you simply could not do the job. Once you've got your first work experience under your belt you will already have a working knowledge of one area of television, you will know some of the major people involved in your field and people will know what your interests are. The easiest way to get out of the industry at this point is to show no enthusiasm for the media – to effectively sit in the corner of the production office and not contribute.

One producer told me the industry was surprisingly close knit – everyone does know everyone else – or at least will know someone who knows someone else. If you get a reputation for loafing around, complaining about making more cups of tea or having to carry out menial tasks, that reputation will go before you and pretty much see to it that you never work in television again. By the same token, if you work wonders in your job – excel at what you do and do far more than is reasonably expected of you – you could find companies falling over themselves to get you on board.

Another freelance production worker explained to me that there's always someone involved in a production who holds the whole show together – they provide an area of complete calm and control in the frantic sea of work around them. This person is usually an assistant or a secretary, someone who doesn't have a high-profile job, but without whom the production would fall apart. Then there are the brash, extrovert, loud-mouthed employees who make an extremely big deal of every task they do in order to get a programme together. They may or may not be effective at what they do, but they want to make sure everyone knows exactly what it is they are doing. The problem is that the calm worker is the person who should be employed by the industry, but too often they are ignored because of the racket made by the latter kind of employee. Your key to success in the industry is making sure people remember who you are. To do this you have to find the middle ground between these two employee types – do your job efficiently and effectively, be a laugh and enjoyable to work with, but don't go around with the belief that you are God's gift to television.

Word of mouth

Progressing through the industry is really where contacts are necessary. Again, it's a combination of who you know and the skills you can offer. Practically all the individuals I spoke to during the course of research for this book had achieved continual employment through personal recommendation rather than through application forms. And recommendations only come as a result of determined hard work. As the industry is made up of freelance workers the onus will be ever more on the individual to find the right opening and create their own career. You cannot rely on the hand of god, a production or personnel manager to promote you to a higher level or to more interesting work.

A television production assistant I spoke to explained the best steps in her career came as a result of inviting people to lunch simply to discuss television. She'd been working as a secretary in a number of production offices, and used this time to get to know the important movers and shakers in the industry. She worked hard and efficiently at her job and gained an excellent reputation. She admits she hated some of the people she worked for but always kept herself in their good books because of the contacts they could offer her.

Through working with these people she got to know other producers and was able to arrange meetings with them at which she could discuss general trends within the industry and her own ambitions. There was no overt selling of herself or trying to get a job with them, it was just an exercise to let them know who she was and what she could do. They would usually result in another short-term contract.

Half the time you won't even be aware your personal contacts are working in your favour. One television presenter was approached by another programme producer when the producer saw him interview a relative on TV. A casual conversation between producers led to one editor being offered work on a full-length drama having worked solidly in documentaries up until that point.

To the outsider – and for many insiders – this is perhaps the most unappealing aspect of the industry. The need to get in with the in-crowd, be seen in the right places with the right people, scratching the right people's backs to line up the right jobs – it can all appear seedy and sordid. But what do you expect? Creating a television programme is a confidence trick: someone proposes an idea and has to instil the confidence of a broadcaster that the show will be popular. The producers must be confident they can get the right personnel to make the programme. The presenter must have the confidence to do something special with the material and so on right up to the advertisement trailer which will confidently tell the viewers they have to watch the programme. There are so many areas where things can go wrong: people only want to work with people they know and can trust because then they can have some certainty that the show will be delivered.

Identity crisis

Success in the industry requires building up a strong identity for yourself in whatever you do. This can sometimes mean refusing to do work which does not meet your standards or fit your particular style. One presenter landed a job for a daytime show, but as the time for production grew closer he became increasingly uncertain of the material and the programme's content. At the last minute he pulled out. The move certainly did nothing to aid that presenter's standing within the production company, but he felt that doing the show would ultimately have done his career more damage than not doing it.

Refusing work can be extremely difficult – especially given the unemployment levels in the industry – but the same thing applies for production and post-production work. Stick to the type of work and programmes you want to make and make sure you are involved with quality programmes. On the one hand, a recommissioned series can constitute an entire career, while on the other hand a turkey could make your name dirt for ever.

When starting out do not become permanently hooked on work experience. There are many companies which will readily give you all the crummy jobs to do, together with a host of promises that one day your dedication will be rewarded. Make sure those promises are kept and you get your reward. If you work on one series for no money make sure that for the next series you are paid. If you are involved with a company or series for a longer period of time make sure you are being paid after six months at least. After this time it is obvious that the job you are doing is a necessary one and the company should therefore recognize this.

The choice is yours

But what happens if the stress and insecurity of television work eventually grinds you down?

To begin with, working in TV can lead to all sorts of work in other media. Many TV presenters have gone on to present training or public information programmes which have never seen the light of the public's TV screen. Cultivating a public persona can lead to promotion work, public appearances, and performances in radio and the theatre – all of which offer different challenges, but do not necessarily bring with them the intensive strain and unique stresses of TV.

Corporate television – training videos or programmes commissioned by companies for use within their own company – can also offer challenges to technical TV workers. Some production companies are run exclusively for the corporate sector. In general these are smaller operations and can offer directors the chance to script, shoot and edit programmes commissioned by companies and organizations. John Cleese has produced many videos on business management issues. Other celebrities have contributed to medical videos which help to explain illnesses to patients. There are even interactive videos which offer the viewer a chance to select the outcome of a particular scenario and then play the video to see what happened next. It may not seem as glamorous as actually appearing on national TV, but they are still lucrative markets, requiring camera operators, editors and sound engineers.

The video games market and Internet technology is also opening up to TV workers. Some video games feature live action, requiring the full services of a camera crew, but equally writers, directors and producers have useful skills, and experience for putting together the story line for a game. Internet technology is creating the possibility for individuals to broadcast their own TV shows across the Internet. With faster communication times video and audio material can be channelled from a website to viewers anywhere in the world.

Getting out of television for good usually means just that. People who have left the profession have not gone on to find a similar area of work – because there aren't any other areas of work which require those specific skills. Instead, they have taken radically new challenges which sometimes reflect the scale of putting together a television show. One lifelong TV worker left the industry to set up his own cafe and restaurant. Another ended up joining the police force. A couple have retreated to the countryside to run their own farms. A few people I spoke to would quite happily stop what they were doing and just go sailing instead. The fact is that to get into the industry and succeed, you have to talk, eat and sleep television. This obsession takes up interminably long hours, requires tact and diplomacy from you at all times, and yet still you will not be sure that you'll have work in 12 months' time. Small wonder that when people have had enough of the industry they move on to do something completely and utterly different.

The trick is not to end up doing something which you don't want to do. This may seem obvious but since getting into the industry requires hard graft and commitment it is easy for the newcomer to be overawed by everything and lose sight of the initial reason for entering the industry. Instead you will do any work whatsoever that has anything to do with programme making.

No matter what work is offered to you make sure it is what you want to do. It will be a waste of time and resources training yourself to work on location just to find that you hate this work. Before you set out on the road to employment in television see if you can shadow someone in the industry. Alternatively ask to sit down and chat to them about what they do and make sure you know what you're taking on. No matter what you end up doing, no matter how little you're paid or how much time the job consumes, you must always keep an eye on your ultimate aim. You must know the position you are heading for and do everything in order to attain that.

Appendix:
For what it's worth

Television will not immediately line your pockets. In fact, it's more likely to plunge you into debt for the first few years. It may still be possible to claim income support while you are on work experience for a company, but you will run into trouble in this area if you are unavailable for work, job interviews or any of the government's back-to-work initiatives. It could be that you end up paying for the privilege of working for nothing.

It's worth noting that in one case, an individual who moved from being unemployed and on work experience to being employed by a production company actually ended up with less money in their pocket. Then there's the case of the production assistant who did 14 hours' work for the princely sum of £25.00. In short, do not expect to receive enough money to live on for the first few months – possibly years – of employment.

Your geographical location can decrease both the amount of money you are earning and the opportunities available to you. Clearly you need to be in one of the major city centres in order to work in a TV broadcast studio. Independent companies do exist in other parts of the UK, but London remains the centre of the industry and in some cases you can double your fee by doing a job in London compared to Cardiff or Edinburgh.

There are no strict guidelines governing how much you can expect to receive for what you do. Pay rates are a combination of the profile of the production – in terms of the company and of the programme being created, your own experience and your status. The latter two may be different things. A presenter, for example, may find that in his first year of work he enjoys incredibly high status and is able to charge £2,000 to £3,000 per half-hour show in spite of their inexperience. Twelve months later they may find it hard to attract work which pays over £100 for them to turn out. In production it's generally the case that the more experience you have in a role, the higher the fee you can charge.

It is possible to obtain year-long contracts for television research positions or in general programme development. Do not expect your first salary to be above £12,000 in this instance. Otherwise you will be expected to negotiate your pay on a weekly or daily basis according to the type of contract you are signing. BECTU (the Broadcasting Entertainment Cinematograph and Theatre Union) publishes a range of minimum rates for the job. The rates are daily and weekly, and rise according to the number of hours worked each week. Runners are not included in the pay scheme – it appears they must either make their own arrangements or accept that such work will be carried out as unpaid work experience. People in the industry agree this does verge on exploitation, but it must be remembered that there is no other way to find out how the industry works and to get meaningful experience. It should also be noted that the names given to certain roles sometimes differ between production teams – as do the specific tasks expects of those people.

A location assistant can earn anything up to £800 per 72-hour week – that's 10 hours per day, 7 days a week or over 14 hours for a 5-day week. A location manager can expect roughly £200 on top of that. An experienced clapper/loader can command around £700 per week, while skilled camera assistants – grips and focus pullers – will earn almost £1,000 per week for the same number of hours. The role of assistant editor starts at around £350 for a 40-hour week, rising to over £700 per 72-hour week. There are additional payments negotiable for location work inside and outside the UK, travel time and unsocial hours.

Professional researchers in television can earn £800 per week (72 hours) rising to over £1,000 for a senior film researcher. A skilled lighting director, camera operator and costume designer will also be able to charge upwards of £1,000 for a 72-hour week.

It's worth bearing a couple of things in mind here: First, you will not be able to earn anything near these kind of rates for your first ten years in the industry. These rates presume the worker is fully skilled, professional and has the experience to prove it. It is more likely that you will start off earning, say, £60 a week, rising to £100 to £200 after six months and possibly reaching £300 to £400 per week after four or five years. Of course, you may be a high flyer or be able to get yourself on to projects which do pay higher rates – but be realistic.

Secondly, the reason why many of these people can charge over £1,000 per week is because they will not be working every single week in the year. You may be excited by the prospect of working a 12-hour day as a camera operator and taking home £200 to £300, but you may not work again all month.

You will have to negotiate your own rate for your job at every step along your career – and you may find that people in a similar position to you are paid more (or less) simply according the type of bargain they have been able to put together with the production manager. As you rise in your profession you will find it easier to negotiate your remuneration and you may even find there are some projects you are willing to do at a lower rate, because they seem particularly exciting to you.

Don't forget, if you are going to work freelance throughout your career – or even if you anticipate working through a number of short-term contracts – your remuneration will have to be sufficient to provide your own holidays, pension scheme and sick pay.